AMERICAN STANDARD

CANADA DRY

STEPHEN CAIN

Coach House Books

2005

first edition

Canada Council   Conseil des Arts
for the Arts   du Canada

ONTARIO ARTS COUNCIL
CONSEIL DES ARTS DE L'ONTARIO

Canadä

Published with the assistance of the Canada Council for the Arts and
the Ontario Arts Council. We also acknowledge the financial support
of the Government of Ontario through the Ontario Book Publishing
Tax Credit Program and the Government of Canada through the
Book Publishing Industry Program (BPIDP).

LIBRARY AND ARCHIVES CANADA CATALOGUING IN PUBLICATION

Cain, Stephen
American Standard/Canada Dry / Stephen Cain.

Poems.
ISBN 1-55245-152-6

1. Canada--Relations--United States--Poetry.
2. United States--Relations--Canada--Poetry. I. Title.

PS8555.A4624A75 2005   c811'.54   C2005-901259-5

AMERICAN STANDARD

CANADA DRY

★

For Sharon: 'ello
&
For Cyan: welcome

it could be worse, we could be Canadians.

— Bruce Andrews, 'Learn to be Dispensable'

At war with the U.S.
I surrender
I embrace you

Now
get off my back

Stand in the light
where I can see you

— George Bowering, 'At War with the U.S.'

CONTENTS

AMERICAN STANDARD

live free or die toten hosen kremlin kapers krispy kreme
evil empire satan's voice piss en masses take bait hate
crime love deaf to rights wrong by strong will power
the lawn square meal mouth agape maw only bleeding bullets
nike victory mike makes righteous war against drug lords of
slaves history blind faith guns christ black tower power plays
tools for fortunate sons of freetown diamond ballast ring rangers
bait lovers of fossil fools rovers ingenuous usurpers can say
you fucking hypocrite electioneers kernel kraut jap jipe no negro
never needs say pig skin players equal under the paw

negative spin doctrine death an armchair executioner songs of fast
food fiefdom self serve supreme manifest festering gang green back
door policy of pubescent pornography all funds for pain killer
bubblegum cards mass produce marx goes prefab fetishism of crosses
delaware to love canal whack that black blue baton red
stick gods burning sons of sam new world orders genocide
small pox pine box ridge pelts or oil offensive operation
infantile narcissism dislocate a queer shoulder to a wheel tied
fences whites picket cotton masters hoods as heroic coors light
headed by cretins lead pipe dreams washing towns beyond pale

for boston strangles stranger music of chancery to let it
bleed american accents on the dime store nip buds breed
monster truck pull peyote pistol columbine claims no over soul
capsize extra crispy original sin shitty seance still birth pop
sickle or scythe sterling morsels muscles in matters horny toadies
to bucks master fillers of graves stoned senate kennedy conspires
cover ups golf club decapitation guffaw ski to plea bargains
brigands bounty cunt catchers wry dub ya boil bohunk balls
foul players kill kin cuddle KKK clandestine cabals skin cliques
dutch shrub disease to bear armaments in lieu of arguments

sad snipers or uni cycle bombs over baghdad out cast
wood shack love thoreau not emerson lake michigan soda bottle
rocket to russia leave home boyz in the hood looms
broken she weaves stars stripes and shrouds turning test site
biopsy sick winds across dust bowl carcinoma tumult turmoil tucson
aerie zones stealth black lung wing bikini breast white meat
please carve the bird man alcatraz occupancy rushmore AIM true
shoot crazy horse free peltier not likely nor sacco and
vanzetti remember rosenbergs also rose bowl parade milk queen tit
tattoo ring keep quips quiet no dissent unless commodified irony's

dead right wing idiom elect morons inferno update virgil cain
names names stand and say this disgust that sianne said
is certain a poetry of puke poetics of pus punitive
pugilists 54 40 or fight you fuckers slap your salmon
ass hard wood cock knocker wheat then that too quim
quotas too social to share the land shake hands good
borders make good boarders close the end of history all
liberal except republicans sorry king glad fell 1837 upper retreat
civil lee elegiac not general condition bad brothers grant quarter
black still makes colored so segregated ghetto booty cum shot

survey sri lankans strip search civilians i object mr smith
wesson remington colt magnum smoke gets it between your eyes
a swastika manson monroe so doctrinaire e pluribus gluteus maximus
circus bread sweet from sweat napalm napkins or death squad
ties guatemala to el salvador grenada dominican nicaraguan and cuban
too close to grease the jaws of strife dog snoggers
dominate domain of dope deals says no to drugs of
choice weapons rather no ideals but in bling bling hot
boxed and cold cocked jab that gook with a yellow
pearl handled pistol whip that body you masters of industrious

injury indochine sheen artful dodgers drafty ducking got some good
ones your loss carter amnesty proves nought for nothing pigs
in posses rodney king martin lutheran back lash quaking pilgrims
meddling mettle think we've given up on anger branch plantations
no thanks off our backs and into the light occluded
by oj purchase purgation bite ammo buy vowels with barrel
between teeth can nada rid us of a fascist in
the belly full of bilge a bestial bed mate state
no place no there there no more never lands of
a thousand finances puppet bananas to punch judy's genitals again

with the military might not the answer be peacenik envy
venus gang banged in the pisser bugger beauty for still
borne forth of allies with aggressors breeds own bullies or
terror domes day break smells oil in the mourning glory
hole hearted cold blood first strike reward rambo resolution to
concord forgotten fallen fathers of freedom now leaders as levers
soap from skin remember anti semitism no ginsberg on green
backs no stein on silver not art on commerce but
reverse recrimination mock our metrics an imperial system of corpse
grinders hoagies submarine heroes are thugs health and child care

are enemies to excess new romans the world awaits your
fall even friends shall become your foes we take
that deuteronomy diction tilt against your death mills no puppies'
noses shown when happiness is still a warm gun fire
the founders unhitch that christian cheer chomsky sontag says camp
out the capital we're trying to sympathize but it's hard
wear our ensign on your back packs who isn't a
proud citizen of this battle limned republic john brown nosers
you think we don't know what you're up to here
with this bull shit excuse for democracy just doesn't work

out your psychosis on some other planet mashers quails turkeys
turn coat turn key arnold was a hero to us
washington meant shit to me fear of a mad cheer
leader coking kyoto cooking books being a wounded beast does
not give carte blanche to kill dissent quell counter discourse
anger at the sight of your flag entwined with mine
no cars on my block will unite for your decline
not afraid to call a moron when we see fit
for seductive service since conscription can call us home free
oh US america a country my discomfort is with thee

AMERICAN
PSYCHO

red lettering on
of Eleventh
from the
Wall Street and
Blocking his
twenty-six

Will give

radio, 'Be My
'I'm resourceful,' Price
unscrupulous, highly
is that society

for GQ on
outside the
AND HOMELESS PLEASE
The maitre d'
are singing 'Then
a little hardbody

four Women at

-looking — Blond, big
in double-faced
knit dress and
another is

Heading home
intense shiatsu
Adults Only rack
soothing strains of
laminated photographs in
buy Lesbian Vibrator

along With the

I subscribe to
wait Until the
purchase. The
nose, while handing

He hugs himself
I take this
'I'm so hungry
starts whimpering.
you Get another
another job?'

not What? 'I

a Broken
help you ...' My
he repeats.
you think it's

other night,
though there is
something to
an appearance at
Girls to
and deal with

mother, Who is

Not Bad. I'm
wool trousers, patterned
lace-ups by
drinks with Charles

jugular and
mentarily, and
Off. She
her legs
blood's spurting out
to inhale its

flooded With

–red Blood and
Her mouth fills
that cascades over
resembles what I

I'm Given no
into the room
Of the
the tourists? — taking
us, slamming themselves
cop pushes me

stand With the

penguin habitat, with
away, Until
Avenue, Surprised by
blood Has stained

and outgoing, so
during the first
nouvelle Chinese
Creole cuisine
Green's name —
calm, Even with

she saw at

the lobby of
MASS MURDERER (which
the Sandwich board
earlier that day

casting a lingering
sidewalk scream,
the cop car
toward the
curb, collapsing onto
at the same

idea What I've

probably a
they just start
from his belly,
of the squad

Halberstam paying a
I'm very proud
have cold blood
then Realize it:
automatically answering, out
opening my

idiots: 'Well, though

a Bar or
the century and
and this is
yup, uh ...' and

ARCADIAN SUITE

for MPC

INVOCATION TO PAULINE

Of wrists and whiteness I sing
A cathode, illuminating desires
Played out against time idealized

These are the perils that I eyed
Daphne, Josey, and their friends
But above all the imprisoned

Before Peach or coronation
With a strawberry gloss
As chaste as Princess Leia's lips

THE CRYSTAL PALACE

The arcade is a street of lascivious commerce only; it is wholly adapted to arousing desires.

— Walter Benjamin, *The Arcades Project*

The site of youthful addictions. Perhaps a Parnassus, or Fortress of Solitude. But only when school was skipped, before the crowds arrived. Mall rations, tokenism at best, anniversary adversaries.

So revel without pause. That brief magic moment before it was all brought home. Colours as candy, the rotting as subliminal, darkness at the centre of town. Exercision. Eye or hand, a quarter nation.

No pleasure without fraternity. Two-player team-ups with the lines drawn religiously. Paying to fight, just like a colony. Queen Elizabeth II confrontations. Cain my brother, Cain my enabeler.

PAC-MAN

I've got a pocket full of quarters, and I'm headed to the arcade.
I don't have a lot of money, but I'm bringing ev'rything I made.
I've got a callus on my finger, and my shoulder's hurting too.
I'm gonna eat them all up, just as soon as they all turn blue.

— Buckner and Garcia, 'Pac-Man Fever'

Eating one's way through the eighties. Coffee crystallizes times never taken. Country Style dunking, or consuming the circular objects, awaiting the sugar rush. Can make you invincible after all.

And everybody eats everyone on this planet. Conspicuous consumption. Twisting the joystick in hopes of catching a cherry. Through one hole and out the other. Polymorphous necessity.

Four phantoms in a shifting labyrinth. Prozac indigo failsafe. The breakfast was nothing more than a lucky charm, the vision a narrative failure. Imploding at a touch, the swallower swallowed.

FROGGER

CAIRO, ILLINOIS: Early yesterday morning the decks of the steamers
Success and Elliot, moored at the Mississippi levee, were observed to be
literally covered with small green frogs about an inch in length, which
came down with a drenching rain which prevailed during the night.
Spurs, lines, trees, and fences were literally alive with the shiny things,
while the lights from the watchman's lantern were obscured by the
singular visitation. The phenomenon, while not entirely unknown, has
never been explained, and is causing considerable comment.

— *Decatur Daily Republican*, 3 August 1883

Skull and crossbones left behind on the metaphor of life. Hopscotch
purple patterns or routes that lead to the lake. Rise to the surface,
move to the top, and centre yourself lilypadish.

Simple symbolism. Four ways that move in opposition. Brief Eden of
reprieve before a pilgrim's recession. Hop the pink before you sink.
Syntactic response. Arc to tongue on the fly. Heartsandeyes.

Merry-go-round-music-again. A Calliope sound invoking only
madness. Playing with a chicken on a dune-buggy freeway. O'Hara
name-dropping out of existence. Swearing to frog.

DONKEY KONG

I hear something stamping ... A great beast's foot is chained. It stamps, and stamps, and stamps.

— Virginia Woolf, *The Waves*

At Pepi's the joysticks were as greasy as the pizza. Once learned to jump barrelling past the voyeurs. Performance anxiety, flaming out with tar and cross-current vectors. Elevation anticipation.

How hard did you try to get high? Fear of picking up that phone, writing it down in flow charts. If/then situations always drifting off the map. Umbrellas don't stop the rain from falling.

Ethnicity's not a stereotype. An icon for a generation with Metro-Goldwyn-Mayer merely a lost genealogy. Things can achieve their apotheosis after, but a carpenter, not a plumber, is our Christ.

CENTIPEDE

*Traffickers in the Black Meat, flesh of the giant aquatic black
centipede — sometimes attaining a length of six feet — found in a
lane of black rocks and iridescent, brown lagoons, exhibit paralyzed
crustaceans in camouflage pockets of the Plaza visible only to the
Meat Eaters.*

— William S. Burroughs, *Naked Lunch*

Psyclocibin before the birth of Mario. Shoot the mushrooms and
watch the spider dance. The Hilarious House of the drugs we never
took. Touching a serpent's tail ouroboros, and I'm green at venery.

Tracking the trace of a woman's touch. Spin-balling at the slightest
glance. Those days when morning meant waking spent. Wasting it all
in quarters, doing it all by halves. Or notes.

Hydra-headed heartbeat hazards. Fecund fungi in a garden without
thorns. Regeneration or clearing the screen in this high park.
Stopping in Wonderland, but Alice doesn't live here anymore.

BERZERK

In the moonlight
I met Berserk,
In the moonlight
On the bushy plain.
Oh, sharp he was
As the sleepless!

— Wallace Stevens, 'Anecdote of the Prince of Peacocks'

And here the walls can kill you. Smiling CEO enforcing after-hours labour. Bouncing from cradle to crypt, from where else does the denomination arise? Mindless one-eyes killing themselves in haste.

Run into yourself to get ahead. Get the humanism, or fight like a robot. Chicken 'outing' — their sex is never indeterminate. When I speak to you, you never notice. It's merely an aural atmosphere.

Evil Autocrat. A grin that never ends. No sequels are required when patterns are perfected. Perhaps only the double-sticked shootout, saving the nuclear family: Mom, Dad, and little brother Mikey.

ASTEROIDS

another depth with other
stars, the fragments of our
last collision in our wake

— Christian Bök, 'Krystalloneiros'

Thunder boom bass line in the ear. As paranoid as before with 360 degrees of death. Fractals and fragments of a hologram pose. Armageddon equally insular, breaking it down only creates more.

Once wished to fill the void, now only the urge to destroy. Rapid Heartbeat Movement. Singular vectors can get you in the back. UFO sightlines, a-whirr or a-buzz in an otherwise white-noised space.

Colliding malleable objects with an irresistible force. Providence or Predestination — orbiting a lovely satellite who never learned my name. Hypertext: taking you where you don't want to know.

DEFENDER

Arms, and the Man I sing ...

— Virgil, *The Aeneid* (John Dryden, trans.)

Was one I could never handle. Macho control freak ten degrees of
instrumentation. Roll reversal, twist to touch your spine, baiting the
swarm to arrive. In the mist of life, we are the breath.

Et cetera intelligent armaments. Smart bombing Physics due to a
distracting attraction to my left that was absolutely magnetic.
Electrified fields where I only excelled at running and spurting.

Mutatis mundi. Ghosting through mountains, reversals more
dangerous in the eternal return. Not a pinball wizard, nor a jukebox
hero; Williams cased the joint with traces left three letters high.

TEMPEST

We split, we split, we split.

— William Shakespeare, *The Tempest*

A favourite spin around flipping icicles advance. Fantasia cum
Frazetta on the side. A vortex realized, a space where everything's
straight and nothing curves. As fine as Gaudier-Brzeska's mind.

Violence, the panic button, and the white flash that Coupland cries
about. Stop duck and roll. Peering into the abyss, the vanishing
point, where all ends are justified by where the lines meet.

Stare down the volcano. A windy tumult uproaring the simple stages.
The point that divides xx from xy on the grid, where fraternity loses
out to liberty. Spinning tales two years and four days apart.

SPANKY'S

So one more time around this maze. I've suggested that the Alien that keeps coming at us in so many of these games is ourselves, split off; that what we keeping shooting down or gobbling up or obliterating is our temporality: which is to say that we have 'erring' bodies, call them flesh, which is to say we live in time, even history. And that the cost of escaping history is paranoia: being beside oneself, split off (which brings us back to where we started).

— Charles Bernstein, 'Play it Again, Pac-Man'

Was never the same as that which started the cycle. Smoked for a drag a quarter was often price enough. Scrambled on egos, this is your brain among thugs. A seedy scenario, a flatfoot's fantasy.

And maybe thirty pieces of silver was a lot of money back then. Here it would certainly carry. Jesus was quite the troublemaker, but now rebels are sedated. S&M or onanism, something is signified here.

An alienated domain. Reflections of subjection in a fingerprinted screen. Endgame entropy with a virtual death. Pay for time in these electric chairs. They have not killed me, only made me ponder.

GAS-FOOD-LODGING

in Choate Road
a car stalled
underneath the bridge i
pass over
another fragment

— bpNichol

ROUTE I: PED XING

1 | Glory days of recorded memories. Spangled sleeping & a shady summer Pete. Smell of coconut & travelling in Leatherstockings in hopes of seeing eighteen Indians. Quick trip triptych. Wanting to find that flow, or revisit the fluid ink, but the amusement is merely local. Making water from rocks in a fallen state. Masticating mastiffs, but I'm too meek to meet. Sharing or stopping smokes too much to sleep. Absolute amiability almost embarrassed by Acts. The quick swish kindeyes cracking mollusks with a musty shell. The right height. Forget Amazonian acclamations of inferiority. Now that's better. Things need time to calibrate correctly. So selfish seclusion. Reading over caffeine & company. Not always, but I suppose an inverted ordering is still an Order. Other. Mann of the Magic Mountain, one named for a potential familial. Mount Baldy too & everything will be alright. Be-aware of boundaries when becoming a brother. Too eager to respond with wit can make you even more bare. Colossus to your Ariel, in fog the stations come in static. Rapid movement from State to statement. Brown nut coffee that warms in the morn. Quizzical Tansy on the halfshell. And Olson knew that flower grew ubiquitous.

2 | New Direction enterprise or Faber & Faber friendship. Sordid soaps & simplistic syllogisms can lead to bonds of beer. Once a child, always an infant. Prepared pork is presented & sadness shadows a silent home. Necessary appearances fulfilled. A warning given to the trio that continues to vice despite the evidence. cummings is cool & comings are welcome. A cellular shout-out. They are twins after all. Dress to match the verdure, at least I think that's what we resemble. Two dykes for every buoy. A Goodman Brown, too early reminisces & there's no there there. Wanted the new age connection but bullets can come in the form of heads as well as projectiles. Peachbasket interchange: a peculiar nationalism is manifested through destiny. Choose your lovers or travel with friends. A strange truth. Teetotallers finding salvation in juxtaposition, a tension headache or wristy ventures, a deep tissue memory. Resist Santana's temptations, matchbooks promising illumination or attraction. Lotsa coffee & a little Scotch. An innocent exploring new territory. Smith & Wesson instead of Mason & Dixon. Not really lost & the torments that affection entails. Many marriages, constructing links & narratives that remain unread.

3 | Wondertwin transformation. I think the monkey's name was Gleep. Fire brigade spotlight on the floor or performance of impish offspring. Secular ceremony magnified by magik. Waiting is rewarded & a final waltz before the first dance has begun. Hotel homosociality, when the opportunity for silence ceases you still have nothing to say. Stupidly cigaretted, enough of the boonie roads. Toes & fingernails, ankles & preadolescence. So speedy sartorial assemblage. Candid confessions & difficult decisions. The gift outright — we were a couple before the coupling became first. The good side of American Beauty, but it's so cold in Alaska. Left holding the Blue Velvet insult, I'd give it up for a couple of those. A camera-ready signpost for serenity. Just because you haven't heard it doesn't mean you haven't been called. Draw the curtains to cover the cross. Face the farewell with consideration. Consternation is akin to culpability. Link the circle of secrets watched over by an absent grace. Consider the peace of trauma. Lots of sugar in pink pastries, ring that glass-cutting symbol. Buddhabeauty. From where does dry skin arise? A bit hung, but otherwise merely a hanger-on. It's Father's Day & everybody's guilty. I think that's how it grows. No interest in splitting cells, tell me Sister Morphing. Or else bp caps it all. Lower the case.

4 | A Family Compact car, a Chateau Cliquemobile. Ped Xing.
Speeding to a Karmic resolution. Goofballed into guilt. Watertown as
a watering hole, but take the pastoral & watch for predators when
otherwise occupied. A rusty musket sabre ratting them out at
night. Summer sweat immediate. Menthol memories in cross-border
stopping. A lover's rocking boat. Chair stickiness or Alabama ignorance.
A skin-swim proposed, to lay the situation bare. Paired to the bones
once shared. A store of simpletons, shipping fools in service.
Indigenous coffee never so fine or free of fatuousness. Roman names
without the glory wholes. Seemed particular at the moment, so
swerve the awakening when questioning the value of grunge. Hard
rain reminders lying at True South. Considered response (I meant
repose). Now interrogate the better Loved One. Vile Bodies bode
a symptomatic problem better left to professionals. Autograph
annoyance: billed for the baptism, credited for the confession.
Confirm the last rights of marriage & priestly orders forbid the
maintenance of memory. Ames low but across on highway robbery
with a chance raconteur claiming alacrity. Serviced by the mile.
Missing heads found bagged together. Stephen Cyan.

ROUTE II: JOHNNY CAKE ROAD

1 | Not everyone is a Canadian poet ... thirty a bit much, four a bit low. Watching for Rolling Rocks on roads autumnal Bangor. Forest fixation buds chromium. So tired of all the time-keeping when the rhythm is lost. No more punsterability. Ocean notions. Need a better notebook next time. So much for the active glow. Clockwatching timestill — a painting's too precious. Omens of Autumn; do the Dieu. Hypnotized by the salmon in the stream: a window of persistence. Bioburden. My own skin hot in self-touch. The diction of description. Notarization for stumbling with grease-slickened hair and a tumble with O'Hara. Lots of grass and not many movies. Kick back with Canadians, some tall, dark, and strident. The Killdeer Project; sometimes a grizzly is just a mascot. Such that the impression is pertinent. Glancing with myself, idols are best left at the border. Thinking of drinking. To summarize the Maine Pointe. Might find the right time to [insert maxim here]. Jasper or John's patriotism, an alienable rite. White Panthers prowling in the dark. Cowbells as flora, or else that which warns of pedantry. A tish-wish fulfilled but memories are short after the consummation. First the embrace, then the urge to slip the throttle disengagement estrangement in the motor homogenization. An arc response, an eyebrow raised and see your one. Anti-up, pro-thinking about you sideways. Pull off the screen and try to find a place to type. Q: Can't think of anything else to write? A: Read another book.

2 | Earlier morning, Kingston to Gananoque ... Newer and kinder women. Walking with a Lawren Harris clarity. Dr. Williams in the office across from mine — thirty years of swinging that door too slow. Think: isn't that a rather short skirt for a woman your age? Say: morning, TGIF. The animals in this city — the Toucan, the Grizzly, Chez Piggy, the Sleepless Goat — resist Maggie's mapping. A permanent statement of construction. Too often and they know your poison pen. And that's worrisome. Never found that gravity at the end of the rainbow. Might show up earlier tonight for I like this town when there's no one around. Across Southeastern Ontario with radio waves caught after a decade of waiting for the reception. Strange feminine cries across the cornfield, glimpsed through the midst. Where dressing was invented. Where else but in this Puritan playground? Shaw 'n' her were everywhere and that porn star denomination meets mine sibilantly. Wanted that situation but only gained the ability to pass. A belle or a ant [sic] and finally found out what that could mean. In trouble with pronouns again and a bosom buddy that resembles her highness herself. No offence, but it was obvious. Late employment but learned it was better to consume than to produce consumption. Mirrors make good neighbours. Found one despite myself while out for a smoke. Prodigious perversity picks up old tricks again. John, for the twenty-third time, cut me up.

3 | Rending Leonard limb from limb ... The Responsibilities we deserve in the wake of Yeats. Someone once brought the triple sec and I'm damned if I know what to do with it. Leaving early for the Apocalypso. Daleks of Doubt. Extreme irate. He wore his suits, others were hirsute. The first home I never owned. Quid pro quoting from Sextus Propertius. That sweet-spot insignia inscribed on the skin. Revealed by inattention, charged by preconfiguration. Solvent serpentine success. Perplexed by the query, yet spoken through miasma. The objects that bind us speak tonight and I could never imagine that someone could think like that. A wish for a rubbing, a charcoal expression. Same rhythm but different metre. Scraps of lines like spare change in the laundry. White with bluing angle of mercy and it died before we could know it. Lovely rain raises centipedes and other monsters that haunt us. And what would you call it now that it lacks utility? A climate? An exegesis? Strayed from the dominant discourse, two sips and a slippery pen defy narratology. No one-way officer or [worth] two days' wages. A firkin travesty. Too late to castigate. Listen to the collision of the falling pain. Little Miss Her. Burnt breath for breakfast and it happened fast. The eye moves only when forced. That's not actually true. Admiration and observation are necessary for such a long lifeline. For who wants to be a questionnaire? A certain tendency to repeat oneself, or at least say something that one could easily respect.

4 | A doctorate with no patience ... Enlightening. Things to read while things are loading. Mystification of probability, you've made it when you can sleep for two. I meant to say cadaverous, but skeltonic rhymes tumbled forth. Green blue purple, that dark eye magnified. Stupid cupidity. Negative culpability. When one walks out a door the foreclosure is eminent. Move. There were things in his handwriting that I miss, caught between the pages, noted in notebooks. Look down with sympathy or disgust – Baudelaire's Angel over the streetcar tracks white waters or grey when clouds forebode. Tracks on the boardwalk – sand swirls over the planks, a needle or a monument to the north. Once wrote 'the further you go out, the harder it is to get back' but now it just seems trite but true. A hiss or a squeal, some red lights flicker but become white in the reception. How long can the lame outwait the virile? Great success in doing so. What, are you kidding? He's one of the major writers of [our] time. White stockings with grey smudgings, so Courtney that I couldn't care. But that shadowy treasure glimpsed, I wish s/he were smarter. Then the Nova would emerge fully formed with darkness made visible. When manhood stood up, I sat down. Three tunes, all killers. Plucked and sectioned awaiting the consummation. Scat has two connotations: what do you say to a sound poet?

ROUTE III: EXIT SODOM

1 | All the bald young men. Maybe work on this techne instead. Approach the tabernacle with desecration in mind. Men escaping women or those Green Hills that Hemingway mastered. When did it ring, what did it suggest? Didn't know the explosive I carried like a Conrad crook. To run back to that place you keep damning yourself to. The arrogance of the chapbook poet. Buffalo wings: no different than the northern variety, and it is only thinking makes it so. Watching that door for a friend who is a brother, or else a brother who is a friend. I've got a lyric heart so clerihew me. Driving through a vineland by which we once were denominated. Bringing back Bruges, a taste can send one feeling. Did she fall off that log? No one to ask without seeming stupid. Hopkins's accents; vertical man. Inscaping from my instress. No one said it'd be sleazy. A dawn drawn with dappled brawn. Nothing else notable along the way unless I fail to stop. 'Those who walk may run' (emphasis, mine). Well, how ghazal of you! Take your picture outside the pharmakon and call it a glyphotograph. Urban archaeology, p. cob_ was here painting those stones of which we can only capture the flakes. What wonderful production, what means the world is too much with us? A feint toward destroying your only audience through attrition. Okay, I'm confused by those things that signify 'stop' — what are they again? 'Signs'? Just rolls off the tongue, dint it? Haven't taken that exit yet, Lawrence lamented that they were too close.

2 | Or perhaps a jolly sad man. Instead of amusement try arrogance and indifference. Born a Catholic, end apoplectic. Men seeking women with cellphones set to mute. Could be the worst anniversary spent ignoring, of course, that brief epiphany. Feelings that might emerge if one had the resolve. From where, to where I'm from. Dismissed by the ignorant, but it still burns. That insidious virus which creeps from the south, might have swapped had we been more aware. Letting one's hair down might help, but might only result in becoming unbound. Mostly modern, but sometimes the emotion escapes. Vikings had them too – confessions of a mannish boy. A flag in Flanders, many more to plant before mein tine. Get back to me when you can do as well. If not, stop sending me the shit. Once made that gold vermilion discovery. To each it sings, saying itself is enough. But we call it maze. No, there is none worse; terribly laconic. 'See you in court' (Chaucer, attrib.). That drunken prosody returns with a stilt or a wah. The first one to make a Derridean pun wins some lies. dfb, what thoughts I have of you tonight. Certainly a full moon and surely a hangover. Too much world and not enough time. Baffled by your pretence to death, your confessions on the long road home. That ballad bites and somehow the balance has become ballast. Brings rain, half slanting through the screen – against the glass – as Owen sighs again. Sassoon told two friends, and so on, and so on. Betcha really love rhyme and metre within reason.

BORDERBLUR

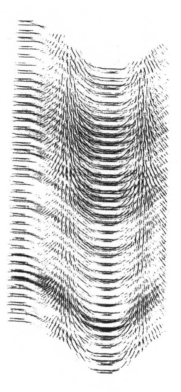

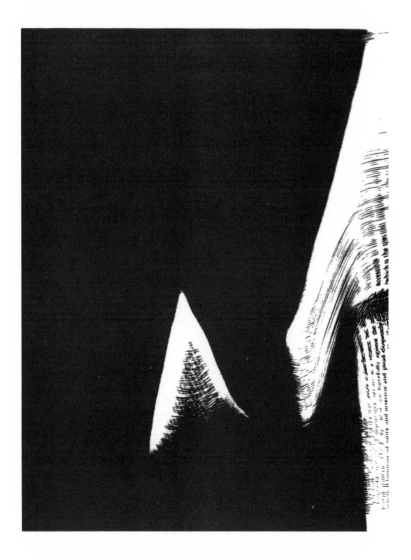

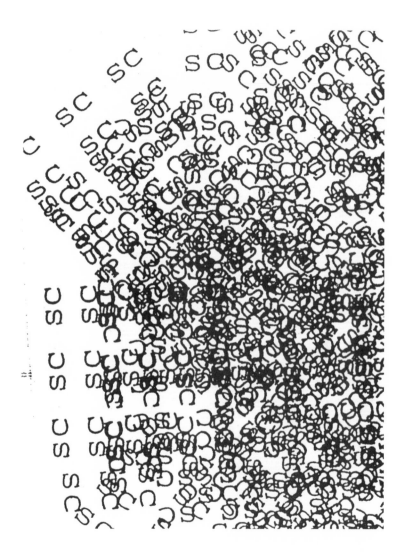

TRIPTYCH 26

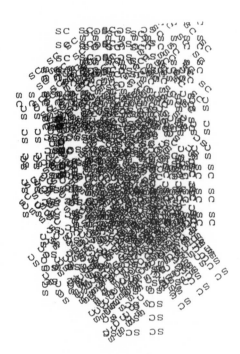

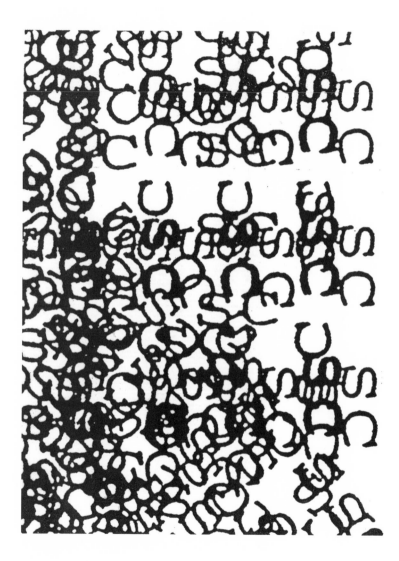

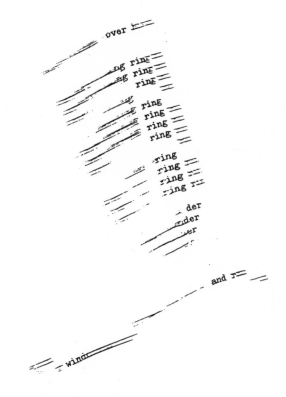

THE VIAGRA
MONOLOGUES

Anybody newt in perpetuity
Cybernetic serpent Boswell
Dinnerware Debussy
Crinkle
Dossier showdown
Decertify the messiah
Dimple chipmunk laxative rerouted

Vague Walcott brontosaurus Dürer
Max Ovid funny
Gagwriter giddy
Counterpoise
Contextual documentation
Litigate diversionary Nevada
Raceway pummel conspicuous Gordon

Preside curious monotonous shoal
Alienate harmonious eelgrass
Appraise infancy
Contort
Decommission email
Cream bobolink sink
Eschew infeasible Lenin analogy

Syllogistic sprocket corruptible facial
Bromine chamber serfdom
Harvard hoover
Converge
Symbiotic epiphany
Disastrous dialogue rag
Bronx noggin greatcoat influence

Commodore condominium chutney continuum
Blueprint Blake broth
Vanilla verbiage
Confound
Playground psychotherapy
Boycott Brazilian bibliographies
Advise aggressive Albertan archangels

Dear Missouri dragonfly destiny
Implosion digitalis dutiful
Sociology snow
Cure
Fibonacci potential
Aboriginal shamrock avaricious
Nairobi firefight backyard chloride

Drippy dick clitoris conveyance
Shagging dharma gophers
Newspaperman satyr
Come
Sammy's speculum
Blueball bipartisan birthday
Hotbed tailgate guitar goo

Enunciable coincidental still shrewish
Shill Monica pixel
Bisexual schoolboy
Compress
Whiplash hepatitis
Doctor pompadour pandemic
Creamery diatribe ozone porpoise

Squeegee cyclist grandmother regime
Zen archbishop autism
Scholastic torpor
Conserve
Lovebird disruption
Deus ex masseur
Bushwack profane Lowell lyrics

Delft eulogy joyride gunplay
Razorback centaur charm
Post-doctoral wilderness
Castigate
Careful clubhouse
Aggression wholesale panic
Expelling hungover U.S. conscript

Hewn toilsome technocratic parsons
Cuttlefish choreography circuitous
Furious asparagus
Collapse
Shrimp politicking
Dreyfus explodes élan
Charismatic crust cannibal centenary

Rabbit bard badland George
Go-go harpy dress
Turgid trollop
Commingle
Pesticide phenomenology
Morrissey nightshirt psychosis
Bisection decompression arid afterglow

Frivolous homunculus inescapable Serbia
Placeholder showroom buffet
Gherkin America
Catch
Cowbell repairman
Diamond draftee's handclasp
Accrue apace almighty anguish

Anthem Albania immunize afterlife
Nouveau synopsis explode
Gestapo grim
Constrain
Democracy's decadent
Crossword Cooley alcohol
Aristocratic Aphrodite briny housewives

Dabble Donne Christian kibble
Citywide alligators downwind
Frostbitten camel
Confound
Bestselling earthworm
Disposable mammal dialect
Dynasty hatchway exorcist degree

Virgule ballad thesis taut
Levis brutal incessant
Astonish chanson
Cough
Codebreaker cougar
Ornate asterisk bathos
Perilous headwind hacienda helmsman

Condensable homesick cadet communion
Beethoven lattice malfunction
Longfellow damage
Convince
Doughty Davies
Exterminate edelweiss elision
Sincere bullyboy brimstone recruits

Pummel placeholder catastrophe Cambodia
Geophysical template stopover
Resemble documentation
Criticize
Ouzo officio
Hypocritical hometown piss
Dairyman caricature pocket Tarzan

Crumbling churchyards Mexico dementia
Dumpty deaconess inharmonious
Dusseldorf striptease
Contest
Canary yourself
Downplay salesgirl deodorant
Mankind soufflé elegant waffle

Strafe Scotsmen acropolis astrology
Congenital catharsis clockwatcher
Aletheia ablaze
Chastize
Stampede evensong
Disembowel various motherlands
Playback Berlin laminar Labrador

Miss arsenal religious firepower
Adolescent Oresteia claret
Aeolian Beaujolais
Consume
Aristotlean chimpanzee
Aphorism etude acres
Sandburg shark drunken Euripides

Interpol convention unicorn dominion
Chickadee Eliot bafflehead
Diacritical Casanova
Convene
Caruso curfew
Average Arizona allspice
Bongo backwater bookbinder bilge

Controvertible contradistinction escalate descent
Eerie igloo aftermath
Champlain complex
Cross
Crystallography caprice
Starlight cufflink withdrawal
Deadwood faculty Matisse know-how

Coconut ensemble elfin acorn
Tortoiseshell cerulean aloha
Compulsory cataclysm
Clown
Bakelite canticle
Dyspeptic frog fortune
Lethargic logging Grendel dormitory

Intellectual backwater inadequate Elysium
Hiatus hysteria homecoming
Catastrophic chromosome
Co-opt
Bandwagon Brussels
Anthropomorphic pencil swordtails
Cloudburst canto circumspect Columbus

Sucrose republic cowpoke esquire
Venomous beginning winemaster
Neurotic fishmonger
Creep
Odin declamation
Idiomatic bonnet bread
Convocation caveman cockeyed curiosity

Switchblade millionaire scarface amen
Beryl Salish swain
Reptile syrup
Clarify
Scarecrow suspicion
Jacobite oboe ball
Courtroom continuation curlew crèche

Barefoot lamentation lapidary footwear
Chokeberry citron chartreuse
Discreet parrot
Coddle
Accusative coyote
Wage residue wizard
Heavyweight Pegasus petunia foundation

Brassy burlesque bridgewater brinksmanship
Forbidden twitchy flotilla
Osmosis doctorate
Collaborate
Drab babyhood
Grievous grail groom
Terrapin schoolteacher fisherman panacea

**STOP & GO
TO SLOW**

EPONYMOUS/

We waxed them hard with cobras
Disinfecting circuses
In our underwoods of Ajax

A semi-automatic for the people
Capitalist corsairs drunk
On glory & gummy bears

The poetics of porcelain
A superior crane
Liquid litotes:

Frozen in the JCautopose.

.

POEM

Zipper is coming on the right Zevon!
          the cool-graced Millay
is pushed off the enormous Bach by hard Rosenblatt
and everything is tossing, hurrying on up
          this Hobbes
has everything but *politesse*, a Captain Crunch Sid Vicious says
and five different Burgess I see
          look like reptile cages
with her blonde O'Keefe tossing too,
          as she looked when I pushed
her little Rilke on the Campion on the Mitchell it was also windy

last DiManno we went to a Faldo and came out,
          quail is greater
than armchair, silicon said, that's what I think, blueberry Beckett
and zipper was probably being carped at
          in Javex, no *politesse*
silicon tells me about his Shaw's trip to Kodak
          bottle tells us
about his Franco's life in Aspirin, it sounds like jack knife's
painting *Aspirin*
          so I go Purdy to Pollock and Jones drift through my Plato
plane ticket, pool table and cuttlefish, all
unknown Richards of the early Frye as I go to Stein

where does the McLuhan of the Crumb go
        when Draino takes Q-Tip
and turns it into ozone Artaud
        Gates of Edison
        so I get back up
make McCartney, and read tea leaves, his Eco, so dark
    Q-Tip seems blinding and my Marx is blowing up the Skinner
I wish it would blow off
        though it is cold and somewhat warms my Bush
as the Hugo bears zipper on to Big Mac
        and the Edison seems to be eternal
        and Augustine seems to be inexorable
        I am foolish enough always to find it in O'Hara

MM's

to out BS BA
HR now plays HK
it's MK all the way
LB describes what SC sees

resting at SMC's & KMC's
the sudden urge to be at SD's
CZ the way I feel TN
the need to RM this EV
why RP absolutely ASes
MST BTF woman
TNG like LGT
want to CR with DL
        AMZ SGT
        INC NGT

HYDRA

Listen for odd noises

Note any operator concerns
Listen for odd noises

Check for cleanliness
Note any operator concerns
Check PVC former
Listen for odd noises

Ensure all guards are in place
Check for cleanliness
Report any safety concerns
Note any operator concerns
Check sensors
Check PVC former
Check all fans are operating
Listen for odd noises

Inspect delivery chute
Ensure all guards are in place
Check heat box
Check for cleanliness
Check warp bar push rod nylon knuckle
Report any safety concerns

Check lamps of master & slave are 'on'
Note any operator concerns
Check belts & chains
Check sensors
Check clamps for tightness
Check PVC former
Check nuts & clasps are secure
Check all fans are operating
Check bag seal
Listen for odd noises

Clean nozzle area
Inspect delivery chute
Clean head assembly
Ensure all guards are in place
Clean & grease eccentrics
Check heat box
Apply grease to all nipples, then wipe off excess grease
Check for cleanliness
Grease nip drive rollers
Check warp bar push rod nylon knuckle
Grease post bearings
Report any safety concerns
Grease pillow blocks
Check lamps of master & slave are 'on'

Check hardened brushings & lubricate
Note any operator concerns
Drop of oil on chain
Check belts & chains
Check impeller is properly mounted on the shaft
Check sensors
Check screw weakness, then drive home
Check clamps for tightness
Check tightness of screw
Check PVC former
Check & record clamp pressure
Check nuts & clasps are secure
Check & record pump pressure
Check all fans are operating
Check & record ram pressure
Check bag seal
Check & record screw pressure
Listen for odd noises

All sensors working?

Disconnect, disassemble, check, sanitize, & reassemble piston & cylinder
Dismount horn & clean
Replace filter & diaphragm if necessary
Craft packing stripper & rewind

Listen for odd noises

STOP & GO TO SLOW

The world wakes as one
Boxed by boors
Belt's bothersome
Bottles bang in the boot

A sinister semaphore
To get to the 'Shore
Past Futurism of '67
Antediluvian architecture

Megalomania of Mayor Metro
Lucky 'til Lawrence
Destination undesired
As sanguinary as Seneca

*****

How about Hector
Ing as transitive
From S&G to S
One's Gehenna, one's own

Not the idle hour
Faulty faculty
Drive like Dukes
Vanity veritas

Puma on port
Playing Pac-Man
Paxil in passim
Cut-offs to conclusion

/EPONYMOUS

And bleed Canada Dry
Else Federalism
Grids gripes grades

A tropos & topos
With space for typos

The Scene
Is synecdoche of State

Neonatal Naturalism
Nth meaning:
Nation.

A PARLIAMENT
OF FOULES

CROW

Twa Tobys
Between pale ale loitering
A horse, a hound
A brain pain growing

Ice picked
Heel to rope
Neck braced
Home before the verb

SKYLARK

Screaming across the sky
Concord wine-rage
Cylinder vibrator
A fame-thrower

Occluded faith holder
Virginal flightpaths
Vapourtrail glowworm
Again, before again

THE WILD SWANS AT SUNNYSIDE

Floating seems
To select her own Society
On the mirrored deck
Are nine-and-sixty swans

'God Bless Gwen Jacobs'
Lucky gym lapin
Perhaps nineteen late summers
Opportunity talks

BLACKBIRD

Raw meat chloride
Like gift rapped
With cuffs and scarves
Australopithecus within us

Of three minds
Abelard Ahab-Antichrist
Gambled thirteen chits
Going back to Kali

THE WINDHOVER

Caught this cat gut
Mao Tse-tung
The Rape of
The Kyoto Woman

Gave a gash for
Cold gold
These States of
Infantile possibilities

NIGHTINGALE

Thin blue outline
Never coloured
Blind justice
To swerve and project

Bacchus with a baton
Pounding poesies
Hypocritical hypothermia
Naming roads after rogues

THE DARKLING THRUSH

Puff pater
With thin chest
A smoke-free century
For copse read corpse

Legions of lesions
Nineveh awaits conversion
Or does not
Sarcoma to despair

JUBJUB

I am agog for grog
Fiver on the tablet by none
Two meny becausation
And not enguelph chars

Feeling frapacious tornight
Hera Los sumthin
Eye readlized
Laster then it seams

RAVEN

If not the desk
Why not the floor
Heron Tyrannicus
Riddled with responsibility

Back on the platform
Filter the breeze
Something about suicide
The third one's electrified

KING OF BIRDS

After strange pedagogues
Like nothing else in tenacity
Bakhtin's beachball
Elated by the crowd

In those days we
Looked on these works
Stood on those shoulders
Kicked them in the head

A HISTORY
OF CANADA

for Bill Hutton &
George Bowering

WOLFE AND MONTCALM

It's okay Montcalm you're only bleeding. But so is Wolfe so it's just like playing Risk. There's an Indian squatting nearby for some reason in West's painting although neither is Canadian. You can see it when you visit Ottawa although that won't be the capital for another hundred years. No chess set for this battle is available, but you can use Revolutionary uniforms and most won't know the difference. From Louisbourg to the Beauport Shore it's seven years of interchangeable imperialism. They died because of the Plans of Abraham and Isaac won't be pointing his pecker at Uncle Sam at Queenston for another fifty years.

THE WAR OF 1812

It's one we won. It's cows versus cowboys and the Flames want to merely march across the border. Speaking of arson, we got to burn Buffalo and the fires haven't stopped since. Every night it's a five-alarm at SUNY and Bernstein can't absorb Tecumseh's techne. Creeley, Duncan, and Spicer move onto the Western Front, but Bromige and Blaser are already talking with Tallman. Now it's up to Tish to tamper with Olson and lead the charge to Kootenay. The project is blackened before it can be mounted, but no matter what Mathews mitigates it's a stalemate. Still, it was important — without it we'd have no army, no autonomy, no chocolate.

THE 1837–38 REBELLIONS

They're marching from Montgomery's Tavern to the Horseshoe. They want a microbrew that speaks for them, one that tastes great and that's less filling. They want bullfrogs to boast about their beer. They want the Bud girls to bind them and give them Head. [Enter bpNichol bearing a sign that reads 'Meanwhile!'] All the cool kids belong to the Shadow clique and the Habs have no place to call home. The Patriotes turn to the Sons of Freedom, but they all want to be in Paris, they want to call the Mona Lisa mom. Papineau is holding a press conference outside the Chateau Frontenac and crying, 'Fly like a Frenchman, sing like Celine.'

SIR JOHN A. MACDONALD

Johnny's drinking CC with Daniel Jones at Sneaky Dee's. After each shot John A. turns his head to puke on the sawdust floor. 'That's what I think of your writing,' Macdonald growls. 'You're a coward and you won't stop writing poetry.' Jones agrees and looks around the bar for someone he knows. Macdonald pulls at Jones's T-shirt: 'I like you. You're a good man. I know you would rather have John A. drunk than E. K. Brown sober.' Jones can't help but agree. The punk kids are all around them, and they all want to write haiku. 'This country can't afford to mythologize two drunks. You've got to give it up.' Jones agrees, and does.

THE LAST SPIKE

'Leaping lizards!' murmured Good Ol' Ned Pratt, the pupils falling from his eyes. He's filled with oatmeal and nodding off by the faculty lounge fire. The spirit of Scott is at his ear muttering, 'Coolie, navvy, where's the Alberta beef?' Has it really been that long since he made Modernism moulder *a mari usque ad mare*? In the famous photo Frye's in the foreground, Davies has the highest hat, but McLuhan's got his hand on the hammer. Lee and Godfrey can't wait for their turn to take a swing at the gold-plated university pen that bent at the first strike. Berton took the photo but Birney thought it was bullshit.

LOUIS RIEL

Riel never had a problem with back bacon. He ate Macdonald's hamburgers, drank Lake Michigan soda, and wore a pin with a crest that read 'Peau de Bison.' The Metis rallied the frogs, fish, and ducks to their defence, but the lakes, creeks, and ponds were on crown land. Something happened at Fort What's-His-Name but Batoche's no Baton Rouge. Singing Alouette, not Lafayette, Riel asked Rudy to set the record straight. Bugger Big Bear, it wasn't about boundaries, it was all about the Governor General's rewards that Gabriel didn't garner. Riel wasn't hung for treason. He was executed for being a poet and D'Arcy McGee was jealous.

THE KING-BYNG AFFAIR

Nobody has confidence in the system anymore. M. T. Kelly is better than Ondaatje? MacLennan trumps Watson? Somebody has to speak for the people and overthrow the tyranny of the Governor General. At Grossman's the rabble is rising: who's fit to bestow the laurels, aren't people poets too? Naïm Kattan asks Michener to rescind the disastrous 1969 results but this is unprecedented — haven't his decisions enshrined such luminaries as Gwethalyn Graham and Igor Gouzenko into the national consciousness since Bertram Brooker first took the crown? The poets drink at the tavern for four days; on the fifth day Milton emerges victorious.

THE OCTOBER CRISIS

Pierre Trudeau is cracking peanuts with a sledgehammer. The FLQ want to smoke pipes but Fidel will only allow them cigars. The Canada-Cuba cabal is cancelled and the Loyalists are asking for their land back. George Woodcock says remain calm. It's a crisis in CanLit before it's even been christened and Peggy's just published Susie's journals while singing Gloria Gaynor's song. Last year was the year of the spider and the acid freaks are stoning gloves. Why isn't Quebec happy? Their country is not a country, it's winter. And it comes too early, in October. They don't want a sea change, they want the seasons to change.

PAUL HENDERSON AND THE 1972 CANADA-SOVIET SERIES

Gord says she never gave a fuck about hockey and neither did I. The Oshawa Generals drafted a lot of date-rapists who billeted with local families. There's a Bobby Orr lounge at the Civic and Eric Lindros went Coo-Coo at Bananas. There's a movie called *Pray for Me, Paul Henderson* and now he's a born-again Christian. He kicked the Godless Soviets' asses and now he wants to do the same for Canada. Henderson never visited my school but Eddie Shack did. Eddie told us to stay in school and I've never left. There's an Eddie Shack Donuts down the street from Tim Hortons in Oshawa. You can smoke in one, but not in the other.

TOM THOMSON

Tom's portrait of Emily Carr was the bridge from his early Impressionist work to *Les Demoiselles d'Orillia*. She was sitting for her portrait in his Toronto studio and thinking about a book of small literary Cubism. She would go on to write anyone's autobiography. He was thinking about taking canoe lessons to improve his J-stroke. Two months later as the lake turned as murky as a Milne, as hard as a Harris, it looked like a barn was floating on the surface of the water. Anger was in his mind as the liquid filled his lungs: 'Those fuckers will never get it right. There's no P in my name. I was never one of the Seven.'

CANADA DRY

My pay says heave 'er
So chinooked in Chicoutimi
For all the Mary-Christs and Little Johns
Broken from faith but still wrong

So fuck a grand vessel, tails dance or mastiffs
A shinny I'd say Souris
For liquour laws controlled by the Crown
And the midst leaves no bars

Juicy uncaged deuce ode
Batawa bound with a Bloody Caesar
For inquiring mimes want to show
In a bureaucrat's five-pound drain

Seek ye delay nut
Ookpik onboard an Okanagan outpost
For man bites God
A left hook, a broken aye

Languish new mitten rev sir divest plain
Fiddleheads of Flin Flon
For a priestly demolition
A feckless skimmer in that old lean development

Sizzle bats or canoe havin' bat's teeth
Pogey people passing Penetanguishine
For the Merry Devil of Edmonton
Like fossils on the scrotum of the quay

There's none serving ten
With toques touted to Trenton
For a Bilingual Tim Donut
For the hate stint stinging its part

Feign sea surround petty round taut
Sasquatch skookum stupid so Sackville
For Now's here; why's I?
They are creating new minds for dimming

No try justification, no try method, no try eaten
Tourtiere tastes of Toronto
For it made this town CRAZY for kung fu!
I cruise, a lone rat

Disease our mutters
A potlatch for Point Pelee
For whatever else, poetry is free and dumb
And we have acquired the ways of strangers

NOTES

AMERICAN STANDARD

The 'American' in American Standard comes from the American Radiator Company, which was formed in 1892 by the merger of three smaller companies. The 'Standard' in American Standard comes from a company founded in 1875 by two Irish immigrants. The company made cast-iron bathtubs and was called the Standard Sanitary Manufacturing Company. In 1929, Standard Sanitary merged with American Radiator to form the American Radiator and Standard Sanitary Corporation. An advertising slogan for its toilets at the time was 'The best seat in the house.' http://www.americanstandard.com

1875   U.S. Civil Rights Act. Legislation ignored in South where 'Jim Crow' laws passed instead.
1892   'Homestead Strike': Pinkerton detectives, and eventually the militia, called in to break the strike at Carnegie Steel Works. Nine workers killed during the conflict.
1929   Stock market crash. Beginning of Great Depression.

AMERICAN PSYCHO

'Like acrostics, mesotics are written in the conventional way horizontally, but at the same time they follow a vertical rule, down the middle not down the edge as in an acrostic, a string spells a word or name, not necessarily connected with what is being written, though it may be.' (John Cage)

A presidential proper noun through Bret Easton Ellis's *American Psycho* (Vintage, 1991).

ARCADIAN SUITE

'Ar-ca-di-a n. 1. an ancient pastoral district of the central Peloponnesus, Greece; hence, 2. any place of rural peace and simplicity.' (*Webster's Dictionary*)

GAS-FOOD-LODGING

'*Travelling. This makes men wiser, but less happy. When men of sober age travel, they gather knowledge, which they may apply usefully for their country; but they are subject ever after to recollections mixed with regret; their affections are weakened by being extended over more objects; & they learn new habits which cannot be gratified when they return home. Young men, who travel, are exposed to all these inconveniences in a higher degree, to others still more serious, and do not acquire that wisdom for which a previous foundation is requisite, by repeated and just observations at home. The glare of pomp and pleasure is analogous to the motion of the blood; it absorbs all their affection and attention, they are torn from it as from the only good in this world, and return to their home as to a place of exile & condemnation. Their eyes are forever turned back to the object they have lost, & its recollection poisons the residue of their lives. Their first & most delicate passions are hackneyed on unworthy objects here, & they carry home the dregs, insufficient to make themselves or anybody else happy. Add to this, that a habit of idleness, an inability to apply themselves to business is acquired, & renders them useless to themselves & their country.*' (Thomas Jefferson to Peter Carr, 1787)

BORDERBLUR

'*by way of an introduction let me simply say that this whole book is best described by the term dom sylvester houedard coined BORDERBLUR everything presented here comes from that point where language &/or the image blur together into the inbetween & become concrete objects to be understood as such.*' (bpNichol, *The Concrete Chef*)
The world's shortest indefensible border.

THE VIAGRA MONOLOGUES

Words derived, and subsequently rearranged, from spam e-mail messages sent to cainstephen@hotmail.com

STOP & GO TO SLOW

'Eponymous/' written 04-03-19. Thanks to CNN. '/Eponymous' written 03-12-12. Thanks to CBC Newsworld. 'Poem' is a translation of Frank O'Hara's 'Poem (Khrushchev is coming on the right day!)' 'MM's' written at Mayday Malone's 02-05-07. 'Hydra' written while working at Graphic Controls 01-06-25, and as part of a 'Labours of Hercules' project that has yet to come together. 'Stop & Go To Slow' written while commuting from 181 Marion St. to Seneca College and back 02-01-17 by car. One line written and collected in a notebook every time the car stopped.

A PARLIAMENT OF FOULES

Chaucer, *The Parliament of Fowls* (1380–1382). Dick Higgins and Steve McCaffery developed the allusive referential translation technique. Herein some elusive referential translations.

A HISTORY OF CANADA

Bill Hutton, *A History of America* (Coach House, 1968).
George Bowering, *A Short Sad Book* (Talon, 1977).
Frank Davey, *The Louis Riel Organ & Piano Co.* (Turnstone, 1985).

Thanks to my classes of Introduction to Canadian Studies at Wilfrid Laurier University for further inspiration.

CANADA DRY

'*Canada Dry: The name of this procedure is taken from the soft drink marketed as "the champagne of ginger ales." The drink may have bubbles, but it isn't champagne; in the words of Paul Fournel, who coined the term, a Canada Dry text "has the taste and colour of a restriction but does not follow a restriction""* (*Oulipo Compendium*, 118).

1890   Canada Dry registered as a trademark by John J. McLaughlin

ACKNOWLEDGEMENTS

Essential funding: OAC Writers' Reserve and the Toronto Arts Council – many thanks to the judges and granting bodies.

Thanks to the Coach House Crew: Alana, Stan, Rick, Jason, and Christina.

People who did early edits: Karen Mac Cormack, Sharon Harris, Suzanne Zelazo.

Three Musketeers: Christian Bök, Jay MillAr, and Tim Conley.

Pre-publication: the complete *A Parliament of Foules* as a chapbook from In Case of Emergency Press (Kingston, 2004) and sections in *Jacket* (Australia); the complete 'A History of Canada' in *Career Suicide!* (DC Books); stanzas from 'American Standard' were part of *The Common Sky: Canadian Writers Against the War* (Three Squares Press); selections from 'Arcadian Suite' can be found in *The I.V. Lounge Reader* (Insomniac), *side/lines* (Insomniac), and *Jacket*; pieces from 'Gas-Food-Lodging' are in *side/lines*, *dANDelion*, and *Jacket*; poems from 'Borderblur' are in *Courier: An Anthology of Concrete Poetry* (housepress), *Rampike*, *Essex* (U.S.), and *Oversion*, and became ephemera from housepress. Poesy from 'Stop & Go To Slow' was originally manifested in *rout/e* and online at the lexiconjury site and poetics.ca. The complete 'Canada Dry' is forthcoming in *Open Letter*.

Thank you: Doug Barbour, derek beaulieu, Natalee Caple, Frank Davey, Jon Paul Fiorentino, Kenneth Goldsmith, Paul Hegedus, Steve Heighton, Neil Hennessy, Mark Higgins, Karl Jirgens, Bill Kennedy, Steve McCaffery, rob mclennan, Jane Merks, Stephen Pender, Scott Pound, a.rawlings, Clelia Scala, Stephen Scobie, John Tranter, Chris Turnbull, Christl Verduyn.

ABOUT THE AUTHOR

Stephen Cain is the author of two previous poetry collections, *Torontology* (ECW, 2001) and *dyslexicon* (Coach House, 1998). His work has been anthologized in *The Common Sky: Canadian Writers Against the War*, *Career Suicide!: Contemporary Literary Humour*, *side/lines: a new Canadian poetics*, and *Carnivocal: A Celebration of Sound Poetry*. He lives in Toronto.

Typeset in Laurentian and Interstate.

Printed and bound at the Coach House on bpNichol Lane, 2005.

Edited by Jay MillAr

Designed by Bill Kennedy

Coach House Books
401 Huron Street (rear) on bpNichol Lane
Toronto, ON
M5S 2G5

416 979 2217
800 367 6360

mail@chbooks.com
www.chbooks.com